Complete, Practical Bitcoin and Cryptocurrency Trading Plan for Beginners

Master The Five Stages Of A Trade

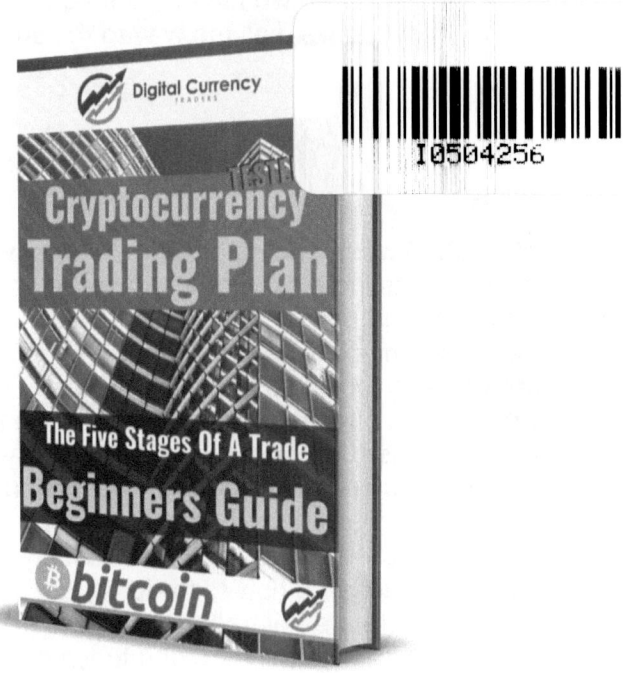

Created by the team at IntroToCryptos.ca

Introduction

The team at IntroToCryptos.ca is happy to present our latest guide for new cryptocurrency enthusiasts: 'The Complete, Practical Bitcoin and Cryptocurrency Trading Plan for Beginners'!
This book and companion webinar, are packed with training!
After a brief introduction, we introduce you to a powerful and timeless trading plan, then we follow the stages of a trade from the start, past the finish line and all the way to the success line!

Finding The Best Times To Buy and Sell

Hindsight is 20:20 when trading bitcoin - in other words, after prices have risen - it is easy to look back and find the perfect time to buy, before the price went up.
This book will teach you how to make money trading bitcoin and cryptocurrencies by looking at the price charts to find a powerful chart formation that often occurs when prices are low, so you can buy before prices rise. Unlike a time-intensive day-trading approach, this book is focused on making profits in just minutes each day, by investing over a long period of time.
Some people may protest that we are releasing this report that makes it so simple to learn how to trade cryptocurrencies. I admit, some of our followers are not happy to see the secret is now on Kindle. But is our mission to share and teach our successful technical analysis strategies - especially to make them easy and accessible for the complete beginner.

If It Works So Well, Why Share It?

You may ask why I'm teaching these profitable trading secrets to other bitcoin traders? We are publishing this simple trading guide because we approach cryptocurrency trading from a different angle than anyone else in the game.

There is plenty of abundance for all of us. Your success does not limit ours - in fact, just the opposite is true. The more people we help, the more we benefit.

Complete, Practical System

Would you agree that technical analysis is a key skill that every bitcoin trader uses when we trade, with the goal of making money? It that is the case, then if we want to successfully make money through trading, it stands to reason that technical analysis is a skill where we should develop PILOT LEVEL expertise, isn't that right?

I couldn't teach you to be a pilot in an hour, but I CAN show you a complete and practical approach to trading bitcoin and cryptocurrencies!
What you might expect from a book on trading, is advice that you should check the fibonacci levels, you should study Elliott Wave principles, you should learn to read candlesticks, look for ascending wedge triangles, bull flags, pennants, and the list goes on...
I find many of those trading guides helpful, but they don't often provide a complete and practical system that follows a trading situation from start to finish - PLUS those extra details you need to complete to achieve complete success in trading.

This tutorial is intended to provide the entire trading plan with options to deal with different variables, and - how to apply this timeless technical analysis strategy onto markets like gold, silver and other markets!

That is our focus at IntroToCryptos - our team of full time traders and trading course graduates love to share and teach our successful technical analysis strategies - and make them easy and accessible for the complete beginner. We also provide ongoing Education with Courses, One-on-One Coaching and with our PRO Trade ALERTS services.

A Simple Trading Approach

I imagine you agree with me that technical analysis and chart reading is one of the most important tools for every crypto trader. And the reason you are reading this book is to take another step toward developing PILOT LEVEL skills...
Or maybe you are frustrated with your trading results, and you are seeking some answers.

Are you overtrading, losing money or just struggling to be profitable? You may be letting losses grow too big, and you may be taking your profits too quickly.
Perhaps it's because you don't have a plan that you completely believe in, from start to finish.
Understanding your trading system is not enough! You must practice it until it becomes second nature - then you will be more selective and more confident in the trades you take and the trades you keep.

And that's what we are going to do in this book and companion webinar!
Let's build a practical and simple trading approach and apply it through all of the cycles of the trade! Be sure that you get all the steps. You don't want to miss one of them because they all work together. The entire plan will fail if you miss just one of the five steps!

Let's Start With Some Proof

Let's begin by showing you some proof that the trading plan we are about to teach you can work, and that you will be able to work it!

ENJ/BTC Before and After 308% Gains

Let us start with this alert on ENJ coin that we published for the PRO Alerts Subscribers. We monitor the crypto markets so our Pro Crypto ALERTS subscribers always have a list of the best matches for our trading criteria. The same method you are learning here today!

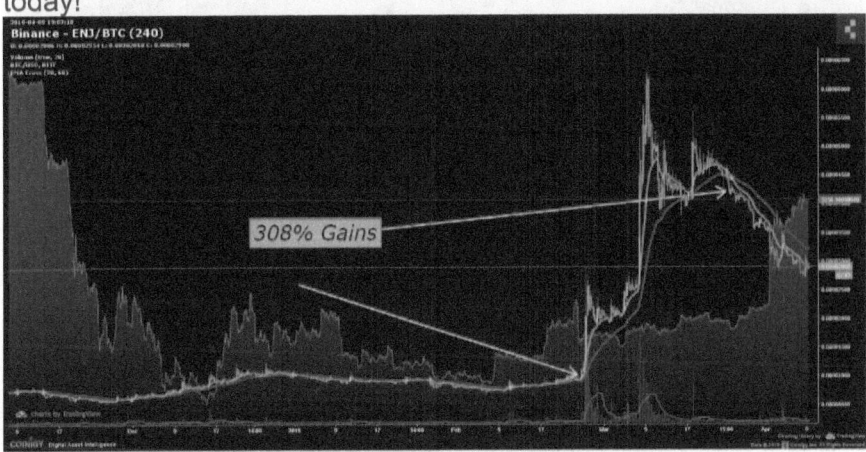

Our ALERT detailed a potential bottom formation breakout above 1032 Satoshi on February 20
The chart pattern and the EMA crossover confirmed our ALERT and the trade remained in HOLD status until March 25. We published the EXIT status at 4218 Satoshi for a potential profit of 308%
This is all based on the Five Stages of the Trade that I'm going to show you today - let's go over another few examples...

DLT/BTC Before and After 147% Gains

Another example, DLT/BTC, you can see that we prepared for the trade entry in early December. The chart patterns were setting up the first stages.

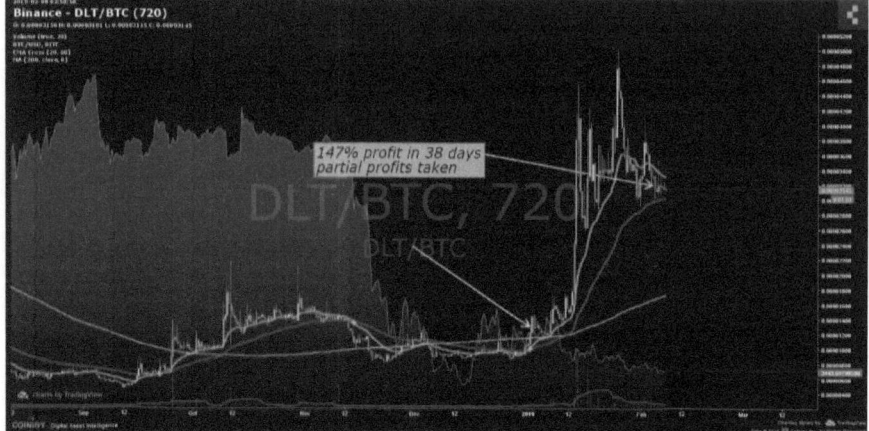

The ALERT status remained active in this market for about three weeks before the chart pattern hit our target entry!

The EXIT signal was issued as prices threatened to drop below the 1-2-3 top formation - demonstrating a potential 147% gain from our target entry price!

STEEM/BTC Before and After 12% Gains

Our third example was a trade ALERT issued for STEEM in February of 2019.

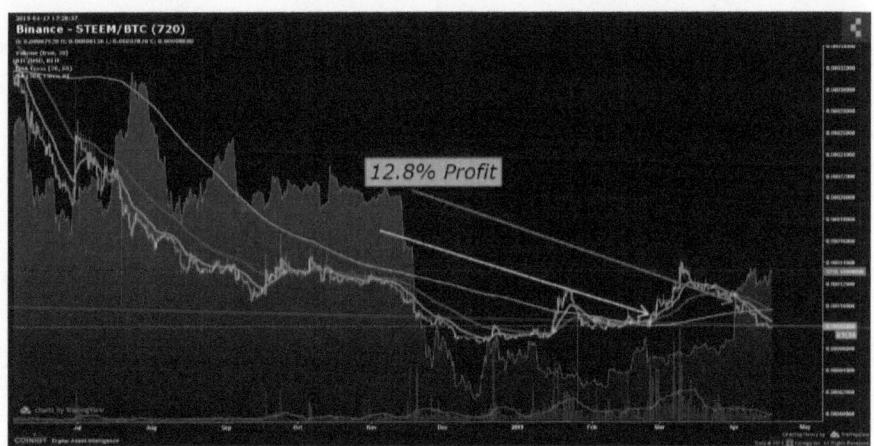

But not all trades blast off to fantastic gains. The approach you learn today includes the all important strategies for risk control to ensure you close good trades and take your profits - before they become bad trades!

RCN/BTC Before and After 71% Gains

And one final example of many, here is the chart for RCN. The general crypto sphere was turning bullish and we published ALERTS for our PRO subscribers as we anticipated several great entry markets in the middle of February 2019.

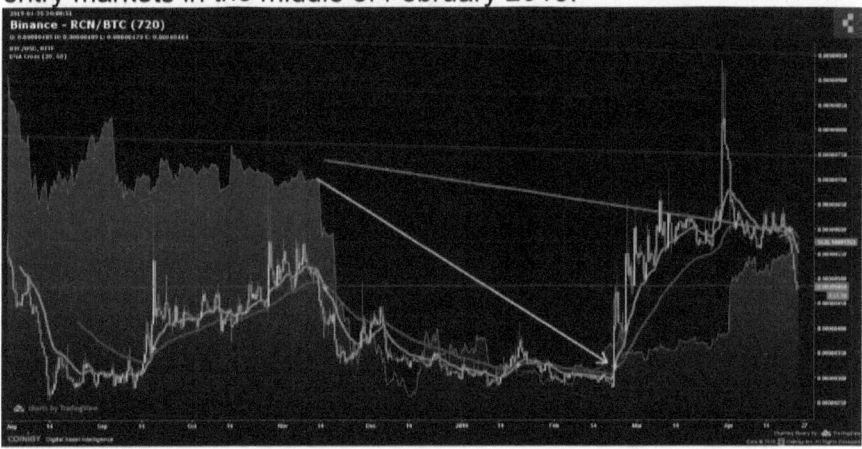

Our EXIT signal for RCN was provided as the top formation broke lower and the EMA crossed negative. This helped our spreadsheet stay in HOLD status long enough to illustrate a potential 71% gain!

That gives you a few actual examples of using the trading plan we share with you here. Let's build the toolset you'll need to identify potential trade setups and be prepared to make money when the markets are prime!

Now that we have reviewed examples let's dig into the five stages of a trade, the basis for learning technical analysis, in a practical way, for the complete beginner.

Technical Analysis = Pattern Recognition

Technical analysis always starts with an understanding of the chart patterns. This is the most important skill to learn. The key chart pattern for our technical analysis is the 1-2-3 bottom or top. It is really simple, and incredibly powerful!

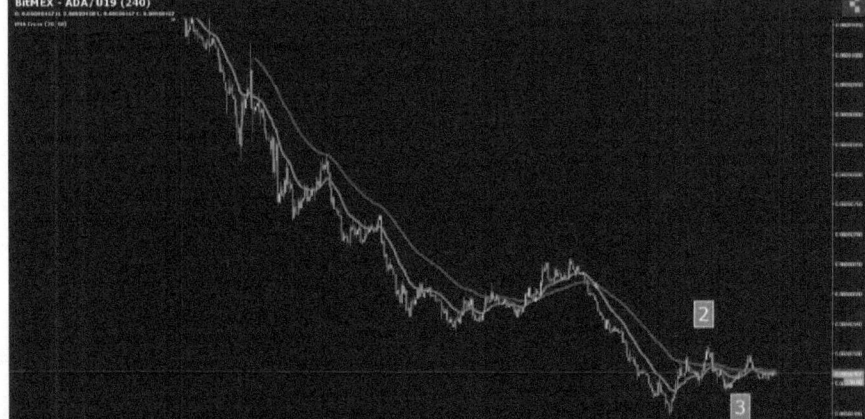

The reason this chart pattern is so important is because it defines the beginning or the end of a trend. In other words, this one pattern creates the chart structure that gives us the ideal point to risk the trade entry, and later, this same pattern also the ideal point for taking profits and closing the trade!

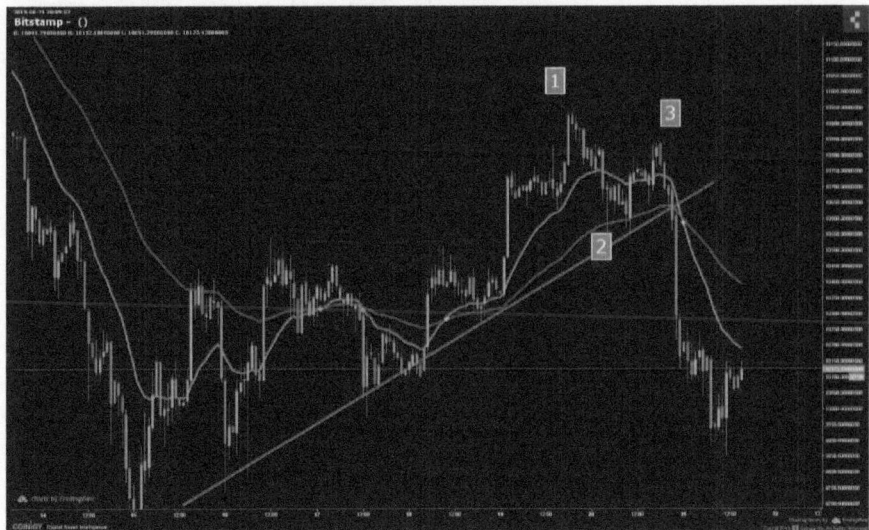

But you will learn more than just the pattern, by the end of this presentation you will have a practical way to look at the chart and actually apply our trading method at the right time.

Why You Need To See The Big Picture

When you see how these five stages of the trade work together, you will see the BIG PICTURE, from start to finish!
- this is where trading confidence comes from,
- this is where patience comes from - you will reject the more risky trades and have the wisdom to select only the best trades,
- this is where your resolve comes from so you stay in profitable trades long enough to get the most out of them!

But first, let's start with the groundwork.

The 'Simple Trading Plan'

This trading plan is based on the chart pattern known as the 1-2-3 Bottom Formation. This trading pattern is actually very simple - and very well known. In fact, real world stock and commodities traders have been using this very same trading pattern for at least 100 years!

Perhaps you are thinking the same questions I had:

> *"If this trading pattern is so simple, and it has been well known for 100 years - then how come everyone isn't using it?"*

And

> *"If everyone knows about it, and everyone is using this pattern to trade - wouldn't that ruin the trading pattern so it would not work any more?"*

Lets review these questions and learn what prevents people from profiting from such a powerful trading signal.

Two Problems With This Plan

There are two problems that prevent people from making huge profits by trading this pattern:

The first problem is: incomplete information - 'a little knowledge is dangerous'.

The second problem is: greed and fear. Also known as impatience and self-doubt.

When I was first trading, I thought that the 1-2-3 bottom formation was an obvious trading plan because I could see this pattern in historical price charts all over the place! This discovery was very exciting to me!

But, as I started trying to make money by trading this pattern, I was not doing very well.

Sometimes I lost money, sometimes I made money - but overall, my cash stack was not growing a great deal. Even though I knew about the 1-2-3 bottom formation, I was still suffering from these two problems - I didn't have enough knowledge, and fear and greed

were working in me the very opposite way they needed to be if I was going to get really rich by trading this pattern in cryptos.
Eventually, I learned how to fix these two problems, and I used this easy, long term method of trading, and without much effort, I grew my portfolio from zero to well over $500k in just over three years! This book will help you learn how to do recognize the same patterns with your coins, and this book will provide solutions to the two problems that hold most traders back.

Three Parts To The Simple Trading Plan

The 'Simple Trading Plan' has been distilled down from hundreds of hours of backtesting and years of forward testing in the cryptocurrency markets.
There are three components to identifying a trade entry point:
1. the first requirement is that the downtrend line must be broken,
2. the second requirement is that the 1-2-3 formation must be breached,
3. the third requirement for a trading signal is the exponential moving average must cross over

Let me illustrate each so you get a clear picture in your mind.

The Trendline

Drawing a trend line is not difficult. We connect a straight line along consecutive higher prices or consecutive lower prices.   As the price is declining in a downtrend we draw the trend line along the tops, as the price is rising in an uptrend we draw the trend line along the bottoms.
Trend lines can be drawn where any two price plates stand out, but they always have more strength when they touch more price points along the chart.

Breach of the 1-2-3 Formation

The 1-2-3 formation takes a little explaining, but once you get this picture you will see this pattern in every chart that you look at!   If you are familiar with Elliott waves, you will know that the 1-2-3 formation occurs at the end of almost every trend, and it is an important component of a head-and-shoulders formation.
This formation is so common that it comes by many names, some people call it the 'W Formation': it is simply a failed retest of a recent high or low.

This strategy seeks a market whose prices are presently coming down to historically low prices. We start off with the thinking that - if the item is at the lowest prices it has been at in a very long time, then the risks of it going even lower are small... and because the price is very low already, we will not lose that much money if it keeps going lower after we buy. Therefore, this kind of market is a lower risk investment to begin with.
As our crypto market price actually hits the lowest in recent history, and we call this lowest price - the #1 point. When the prices rise a bit off the #1 point, and then reverse to start coming back down, we can label that reversal price as the #2 point.
If the prices go down lower than our #1 point - then we start again, watching for the new lowest price and we would label that lowest price as our new #1 point. In other words, the prices are still trending downwards, and we just keep watching - because we are looking for the time when this down trend finds a bottom, hits it's lowest prices - and then the trend changes or reverses... before we buy in.
Once we have a #1 point, and we have a #2 point, and prices do not keep falling below our #1 point - we are getting ready to buy when prices rise again past the #2 point. When prices prove that they are going higher than our #2 point, that is our buying signal - and after this happens, we label our charts with the #3 point... the time when prices broke above the #2 point.
This may sound confusing if you are only reading the explanation without looking at price charts to get a picture in your mind.
This example is the price of bitcoin on Septermber 2 2019

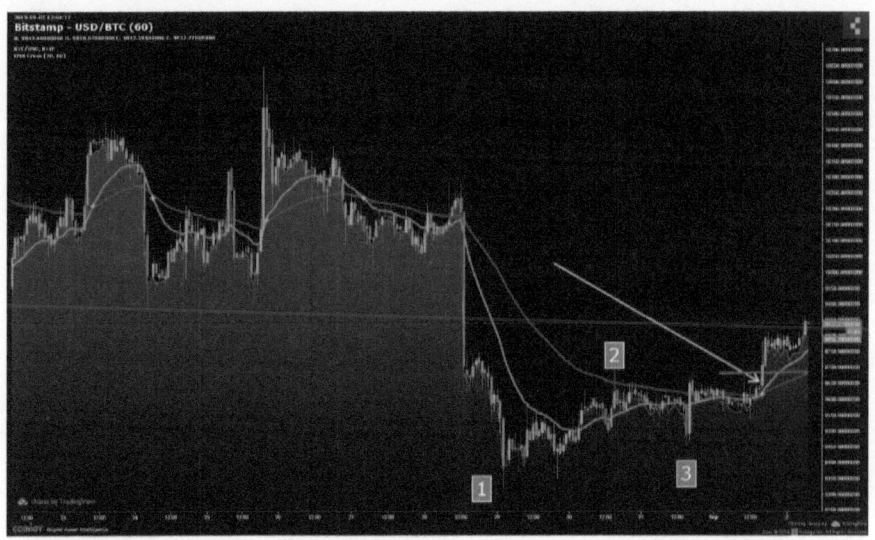

And some updates on a trade that was placed on this signal:

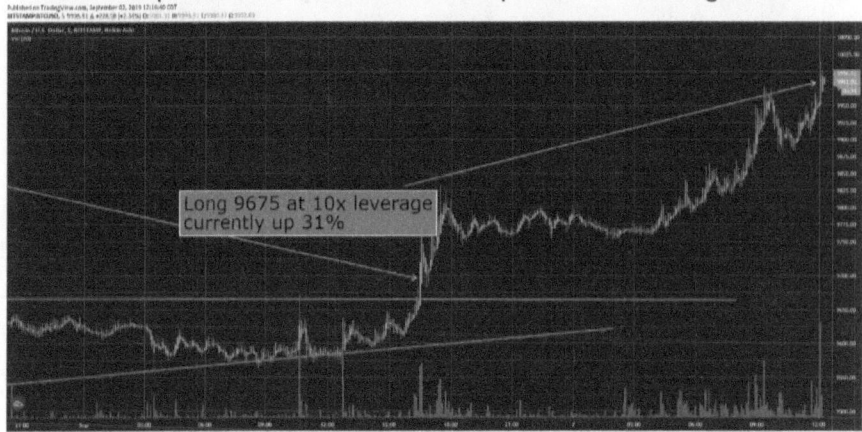

Long 9675 at 10x leverage
currently up 31%

Cross of the 60/20 Exponential Moving Average

Finally, a cross of the 60/20 exponential moving average is included in this trading plan, it serves to filter out the sudden spike in price moves that are common in the cryptocurrencies. These may be intentional pump and dumps, they may be accidental as a large signal group chases a new forecast... whatever their origin, these fast price moves may look exciting but they don't have sustained movement behind them and often fall back.

These short-term moves in prices may be considered as waves coming up a beach, and our trading plan is intended to place a trade when the tide is changing, not when every wave is splashing up the beach.

When 1-2-3 Bottom Formations Go Wrong

The trading method in this book teaches how to make money with these kind of patterns. However, the 1-2-3 bottom does not happen all the time. There are two different 'bad things' price can do to cause frustration and loss of money.

False 1-2-3 Bottoms

Sometimes the price of a coin will be trending downwards, it will come to a historical low, and the price chart will show a nice 1-2-3 bottom is shaping up - prices may even break above the #2 point, creating the #3 point and giving us a trading signal... only to reverse again, drop lower than our #1 point and continue the downtrend lower and lower.

Sideways Bottoms

Other times, the price will come down, hit a #1 point, make a #2 point... only to then go sideways for a long time, with the price hovering between the #2 and #1... never going lower than the #1 point, but never making any gains to give us the #3 point.
The first 'bad thing', the False 1-2-3, is obvious - the down-trend is continuing, and we lose money. We need to sell out of our position, or we stand to lose a lot more money.
The second 'bad thing', The Sideways Bottom, we don't lose money, but we don't make profits.
The Sideways bottom just ties up our cash and our attention, and it is easy to become impatient and frustrated as we miss out on other opportunities.

Both of these situations happen a lot of the time when we seek to trade 1-2-3 bottom formations - BUT, by knowing in advance that these two 'bad things' are likely to occur, we can prepare for these situations - we can expect them - and have a strategy to deal with them to protect our cash stack and keep our money in markets that are rising.

This is always frustrating for crypto traders and we want to learn how to recognize these False 1-2-3 Formation and quickly get out, so we are not wasting time, losing money and getting discouraged... trading in these failing markets takes up a lot of time and attention, and creates small losses.

It Really Is That Simple

That is the most basic brief of The 'Simple Trading Plan'. It should take you no more than 10 minutes a day to manage once you get the hang of it. This trading plan will work on any time frame and it will work in any different market, not just cryptocurrencies and Bitcoin.

You can trade the 1 2 3 pattern in any chart, it doesn't matter if you are trading avocados, or if you are trading cryptocurrencies... You could be trading coffee you could be trading Lumber you could be trading silver and gold, and all of the charts will have 1-2-3 patterns in them, it is a common part of every trend change and price direction change!

Works In Any Timeframe

You certainly can use these combination of trading signals with the 1 minute and 15 minute bars for an effective day trading strategy, but for the purpose of our low-time-commitment trend-following approach, we are considering signals in the charts using the 12 hour bars to filter out a lot of the pump and dump flash moves, and keep us in for the trend.

Prepare Like a PILOT For Their First Solo Flight

Now that we have our Trading Plan under your belt, we can begin to practice for every emergency situation we might face, just like a PILOT would study and prepare before they took their first solo fight!

Mastering The Five Stages Of A Trade

1. Complete, PrIdentify An Alert
2. Alert Triggered
3. Setting Stops
4. Adding On
5. Taking The Exit

Let's take a quick look at each stage of the trade, then dig into more details for each!

1) The first stage of the trade begins before the trade is executed. In this stage, we identify potential chart patterns that may be setting up. That is, our trading signal is almost lining up - and it's time to get prepared with potential entry levels, profit targets, stop levels.

2) The second stage of the trade occurs when the alert is triggered, this is the most important phase of the trade. The approach you use in this stage of the trade can set the stage for your success or failure in trading. This is the most common place for trading errors, and the best place to protect yourself from big losses.

3) The third phase of the trade is a defensive strategy of placing stop-losses just above a new trade. The trades that successfully make it past this phase can become the biggest money makers.

4) The fourth phase does not necessarily occur in every trade, but this is where the most profitable trades will be found and all of the

biggest money-making trades captured by the trading pros likely enjoyed the benefits of this stage.

5) The final stage of the trade is exiting the position. The greatest difficulty most traders report - is knowing when to take profits and get out of a trade. By having this planned in advance, knowing your criteria for closing a profitable trade, and by practicing it, we can be better prepared to capture profits consistently.

Stage One - Identify Opportunity and Prepare

Ok - now let's take a more detailed look at Stage One. It can be divided into three activities.

1. Identify the chart patterns
2. Set up entry, exit and stop loss levels
3. Take a screenshot

The first activity in Stage one is the ongoing habit of scanning the price charts to identify potential 1-2-3 formations shaping up.
Bottom formations in a down trend, and top formations in the up trends.

Most of the time, we can see our trading signal coming for days in advance because our focus is to identify trading patterns based on the 12 hour bar charts.

As we see a potential 1-2-3 formation shaping up in a market, we

- determine what our entry price would be,
- we estimate what are Target profit Level would be,
- we plan in advance what our emergency stop-loss level would be.
- take a screenshot of the chart as we make our plans, and finally,
- plan the stop limit order criteria to ensure we enter as a market maker where possible.

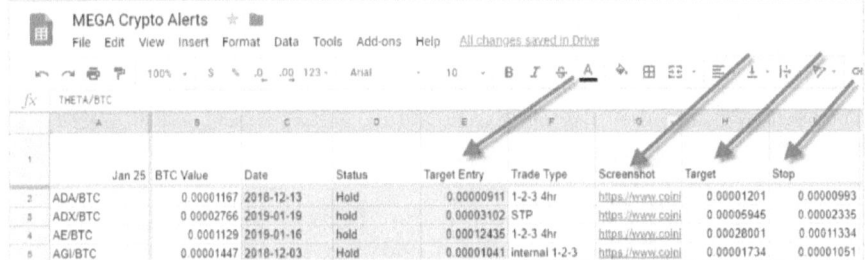

All of this information is recorded in a spreadsheet, so that every trade can be reviewed and studied for what was done correctly, and what mistakes were made.

When you can categorize your mistakes in trading, they are easier to correct. If you cannot pinpoint where you are making mistakes and why you are losing money, you cannot correct it.

WARNING : *If you skip the 10 minutes of daily activities in this stage, you are sure to fail at trading.* You don't need the next four steps, managing your own trading may not be for you. And there is nothing wrong with that. Instead of trading, consider setting up your crypto investments where you can lend your coin for slow and steady compound interest! Visit Coinlend.org or Celcius.network for options.

Stage Two: Alert Triggered

The second stage of the trade occurs when the alert is triggered, this is the most important phase of the trade. In other words, our pre-identified entry levels were hit and we are holding a new position.

The approach you use here will set the stage for your success or failure in trading. This is the most common place for trading errors, and the best place to protect yourself from big losses.

Trading Bitcoin and cryptocurrencies is risky. The markets are thinly traded, they are often manipulated, and subject to uncertain changes in technology, news and government policies.

Your risk control strategy, how you deal with these uncertainties and dangers in the first few minutes of a new trade - will have the most important effect on all of your success. Having prepared in advance, practiced and drilled-for-skill with your risk control strategy has more to do with your success in trading than your entry strategy.

In order to deal with the dangers and risks of trading, we are going to assume that we are wrong when we place a trade, and we only hold trades that prove us correct.

Most people start a trade because they believe they are correct, and they only exit the trade when the market proves them wrong. This is completely backwards! If you are making this error, this will hold you back from greater trading success!

Let us illustrate why..
Reason this idea… if we knew in advance we were going to be wrong when we are placing the trade, then we would make a very small investment wouldn't we? Of course! We would bet small if we knew we were going to be wrong! That would ensure we take the smallest losses.
In a risky situation, we would start with a small exploratory trade, kind of like dipping your toe in the water to see if it's good for swimming… before you dive in.
If we are not quickly proven correct when we open a new trade, then we reduce or remove the position - unless the market proves as correct. Emotionally, it is easy to close this losing trade because we started with a very small position - and because we are expecting to close new positions unless they prove us correct.
Our job when we are placing a trade, is to protect ourselves against losses. If we practice starting new trades with smaller positions, cut our losers quickly and only hold trades that prove us correct, then we are dramatically shifting the odds in our favor.
When we close a small trade that has not proven us correct, we protect ourselves against the risk of the lost getting larger. The longer we stay in a trade that has not proven us correct, the more likely we are wrong and the more costly it will be.

Stage Three : Setting Stop Loss

Once a trade has proven us correct, we move on to consider Stage Three.

The third stage of the trade is also a defensive strategy of placing stop-losses just above a new trade. Or primary job as a trader is: 'Don't Lose Money'. In the worst case, we keep our losses small.

The trades that successfully make it past this phase become our money makers! We don't want to hold anything else!

It is important to consider the emergency stop loss like a seatbelt in a car. We never want to use the seat belt, it's only there in emergencies. It's the same with getting out of a trade that doesn't prove us correct, we do not wait for the market to prove us wrong and hit our stop loss, we get out much sooner because we only hold trades that prove us correct.

Once the trade has successfully made it past Stage 2 and prices have gone our way, the market has proven us correct and we are profitable, but we are still not out of danger.

Our first focus is to move our stop loss above our initial entry to protect our initial investment against fake break-out moves or sudden reversals. Even if the trade starts out positive straight away, we are not out of risk until price has moved higher and retested levels above our stop loss.

Once that stop loss is in place, most of our work is finished.

The reason we move our stop loss above our entry point as soon as possible, is so that we hand over the work to the market.

It Is Not Our Job To Make Money

It is not OUR job to make money… we are handing that work over to our money, we are handing that work over to the market. We are making our money work for us - that means we must let the money do the work as the market dictates.

The second most common mistake in trading, is taking profits too soon. Why does this happen?

If we have taken a series of losses, we may be over eager to take our profits and prove to ourselves that we are correct. We may become fearful of losing our profits and take our profits to ensure we don't lose them... only to see the market take off without us and the mass of our profits are just another 'missed opportunity'.

It is important that you do not mistake your job from the markets job. Your job is to limit your potential for losses, it is the markets job to determine just how correct you are!

The Market Will Tell Us When To Exit

While it is not our job to determine how correct we are - nonetheless, we must have clear and easy criteria that say the market is telling us the trade is finished. I'm excited to cover those details very shortly because most traders report that taking profit at the right time is their greatest difficulty in trading!

But first, a little known stage of trading that most beginners miss and all professional traders use.

Stage Four: Adding On

The fourth phase - adding on to successful trades.

This phase does not necessarily occur in every trade, but this is where the most profitable trades will be found and all of the biggest money-makers likely enjoyed the strategies you will learn in this stage.
Your risk control strategy has two sides: reducing risk, and increasing risk.
At Stage 1, Stage 2 and Stage 3 of the trade, the risk control is focused on protecting against risks, with the assumption that we are wrong.

However, once a trade has approached Stage 4 it is now time to *increase* our exposure to risk - because we have been proven correct.
Fear and greed are natural emotions when you are trading. Successful traders feel fear and greed as well but commonly they feel them at opposite times to unsuccessful traders.
The unsuccessful trader will feel greedy when prices are pulling back because they can get a better deal, they can dollar cost average. The unsuccessful trader will hold a losing trade longer, assuming they are correct until the market proves them wrong.
When the unsuccessful trader has a profitable trade, they often feel fearful that the market will take away their profits and so they take their profits too soon. If you combine bigger losses than needed and smaller profits than possible, trading becomes frustrating and expensive.

The successful trader also feels fear and greed. They feel fearful when they are holding a loss, fearing that it might get bigger. And when they are correct, they feel greedy and they put larger trades on. Over time, the collection of smaller losing trades and the larger winning trades will make a profound difference in your trading success.

Two Ways To Learn Trading Lessons

Through experience.
Through education.

If you stick with trading long enough you will eventually learn to plan out your trades - so that you can identify your successes and failures. You will eventually learn to exit losing trades quickly, only holding the positions that prove you correct, and though hard experience, you will likely develop the skill of putting your stop loss above your entry as soon as you can.
The market will teach you these lessons.

The reason is the market will teach these lessons to you because every time you did these wrong, the market takes money from you. If you stick with trading long enough you will eventually figure out these basic strategies.
But Stage 4 will never teach itself to you, you may never know that you are missing out on the best rewards of trading because there is nothing that punishes you for missing these benefits. If your winning trade are the same size as your losing trades - making money in trading is much more difficult.

The profound power of adding on to the successful trade is not immediately obvious. Without someone pointing out these benefits - and without considering it carefully, you may not appreciate the significance of this common habit of successful traders.

The Pull Back And The Place To Add On

Important perspective in September 2019; we are anticipating a 12 to 18 month bull market run in the altcoins. Should this come to pass, we may anticipate a major surge to take from 6 to 12 weeks, with a pullback that takes 2 or 3 weeks, before another major surge up for 6 to 12 weeks. This pattern may be played out for each of four or five waves – perhaps culminating in late December 2020

Stage Five: The Exit

The final stage of the trade is to exit the position. In my experience, after helping thousands of students learn this method, the greatest difficulty most traders have reported, is knowing when to take profits and get out of a trade.
By having this planned in advance and knowing your criteria for closing a profitable trade, we can be better prepared to capture profits consistently.
If knowing when to take profits is you top difficulty too, it may be because you are putting an 'all or nothing' approach into closing a position, rather than scaling out of your position the same way we scale into our position.

Getting Clear On The Exits

The exit chart pattern should be just as easy to recognize as the entry chart pattern. We should be able to see it coming and be prepared in advance.
Taking action on a top formation is similar to trading a bottom formation. We can exit the trade in stages to take profits as the top formation unfolds and confirms. That is, we plan to exit AFTER the 1-2-3 top formation.
Part of our position would be closed when the EMA crosses on the 4 hour bar timeframe,
when the EMA crossed on the 12 hour bar time frame we close the remainder of the position.

After The Exit

Evaluate, Learn, Apply, Repeat. Have clear and simple trading plan to compare your performance against.

You now have a complete and practical system that follows a trading situation from start to finish.

You have the entire trading plan with strategies to manage risk at the two most difficult areas of a trade. This afternoon, you can go and apply this technical analysis method to any different market from cypto to forex to equities and commodities!

We not only outlined the technical analysis for a specific trading plan, and also provided a practical sequence of stages to actually help YOU succeed when the market conditions are correct.

Let's take a second to reflect, recall that we agreed, technical analysis is a key skill we believe will help us make money. It is a skill we use it each time we place, manage, or close a trade - and it follows that we want to develop PILOT LEVEL skills in all areas of trading.

Do you recall at the beginning of the video, that we said *'If you skip Stage One, you are sure to fail at trading.'*

...and you may be saying… what was Stage One again? That's ok, that's normal. We covered a lot of material here, and repetition is the key.

Stage One is actually the most work you do until after the trade is complete.

After each trade is complete, we want to update our spreadsheet. Update the closing date of the trade and the closing price, and also capture a screenshot of the chart at the time.

Each time we have completed a bull or bear market trading cycle, it is a chance to pause and study all of our trades to find common patterns in our successes and our failures.

We are going a bit overboard here, but we want to be sure you have the complete and practical system that follows a trading situation from start *past the finish line* and all the way to the success line. This is how our experience can become your education!

Our research can help you more quickly attain that PILOT LEVEL expertise in trading, to build the habits and gain confidence in technical analysis skills that really can unlock unlimited earning potential!!

If you don't have money to invest, you are in the best place for learning! Check out our guide 'The ULTIMATE BitMEX Tutorial' on Amazon Kindle and learn how to set up a practice trading account for free and start practice trading! Build the skills like a pilot in a simulator , and when you do have money - you'll already know to keep it and how to grow it!

Download the free chapter from my book, get a free copy of this power point as well! Watch ALL the videos on YouTube!!

Conclusion and Next Steps

We introduced a brief overview of our trading plan and an outline of our approach through all the five stages of a trade!

You now have the secret key to make your money grow like you have never done before! It's simple. It's not complicated. This method of trading does not rely on prices going up and it does not rely on prices going down.
It is easy to do, you can set it up in minutes and continue doing it to make money consistently - whether prices are going up or down!
Once you practice this knowledge, once you know this strategy, You have it. It's yours forever.
You CAN make your money work for you - and it feels good! It is our hope you will follow this good feeling and learn all you can about how to manage and grow your money!!

Success Is A Habit You CAN Learn

When you look back, you'll see that getting wealthy was just a matter of making money, keeping your money, and growing your money. And you will understand: the trouble that most people have - that prevents them from getting wealthy - is they do not have the habit of keeping their money because we were never taught that we can, and should, make it grow!

IntroToCryptos teaches beginners how to trade micro positions of bitcoin and cryptocurrency as a way to learn and practice thinking about money the same way that wealthy people think about money. With practice and evidence of successfully growing your money, you begin to gain confidence in keeping your money so you can practice making it grow. Once you achieve just one dramatic success with this approach, you will emotionally build new habits with money that will enrich all aspects of your life!

YOU CAN DO THIS. You CAN learn how to make money grow, you can repeat the success, and you will discover - it feels good to write a trading journal to keep track of your successes and lessons, and you make your money grow more - it feels good, you feel eager! You repeat this a few times and soon the good feeling settles into confidence. With confidence in your ability to grow money, you begin to meld a very good feeling into the habits of following a personal budget, managing your money, making your taxes more efficient, and growing wealth in all aspects of your life!

In your excitement, you read the books 'Money Is My Friend' and 'Rich Dad, Poor Dad' and 'Think and Grow Rich' - and your life is changed forever.

Gain Greater Wealth, Greater Security, and Greater Freedom

We believe, the habits you learn from following this trading approach will help you build a new and positive relationship with money. You will have a greater feeling of confidence that you can keep some of the money you earn, and make it grow.

By feeling and thinking this way about money, you will want to learn more about money and expanding your financial education will become a rewarding, life-long mission - and that - will lead you to greater wealth, greater security and greater freedom, indeed, to abundance that will help your family and everyone in your life!

Thank you for the opportunity to be of help somewhere along your journey towards wealth!

If you found this book helpful,

Visit the website IntroToCryptos.ca

for additional training for a variety of
short term, medium and long term strategies for trading, investing and lending
bitcoin and cryptocurrencies.

Appendix

Risk Disclaimer

There is considerable risk in bitcoin, altcoin or world market trading, and may not be suitable for all investors. Any trading involves risks including, but not limited to, the potential for changing political and/or economic conditions that may substantially affect the price or liquidity of any financial market. Speculative investments may also be susceptible to sharp rises and falls as the relevant market values fluctuate. Leveraged trading can have a proportional effect on your trading account balance. This may work against you as well as for you. Not only may investors get back less than they invested, but in the case of higher risk strategies, investors may lose the entirety of their investment, or more.

Hypothetical Results Disclaimer

Some trading commentary is based on hypothetical performance results that have certain inherent limitations and may not represent actual trading. Past performance does not predict future results. Predictions do not include the impact of market liquidity and no representation is being made that any account will or is likely to achieve profits or losses similar to those being shown. Forward looking statements include words such as "anticipates," "estimates," "expects," "projects," "intends," "plans," "believes" and are based on this author's current expectations and assumptions regarding the market in question and actual results may vary significantly from those expressed or implied.
Before deciding to trade in any market you should carefully consider your investment objectives, level of experience, and risk appetite. You should not invest

money that you cannot afford to lose. Seek advice from a certified independent financial adviser if you have any doubts.